The Eco-Friendly Shopper

Table Of Contents

Foreword

Chapter 1:
Introduction

Chapter 2:
Nutrition And Organics

Chapter 3:
Organics And Your Health

Chapter 4:
Organic Skin Care

Chapter 5:
Choosing Organic Skin Care Products

Chapter 6:
Organic Bath Soaps

Chapter 7:
What About Organic Gardening

Chapter 8:
Tips For Organic Gardening

Wrapping Up

Final Words

Foreword

A lot of shoppers only seem to have an abstract understanding of the advantages of organic foods and products on the environment and their wellness. Get all the info you need here.

The Green Shopper
Your friendly guide using eco-friendly products in the market

Chapter 1:
Introduction

Synopsis

Organic meat, poultry, eggs and dairy products come from animals that are afforded no antibiotics or growth hormones. A lot of individuals think that genetic engineering is unsafe, unpredictable, and may reduce the nutritional value of food.

But the FDA has stated that the amount of hormones utilized in commercial livestock isn't enough to hurt human beings. As a result, to be viewed as organic, meat, poultry, eggs and dairy products have to come from animals that are given no antibiotics or growth hormones. Commonly organic fruits and veggies, milk, eggs and meat products are produced inside a 50-mile radius of their place of their final sale.

The Basics

Organic produce refers to veggies that are raised without the use of chemicals or pesticides. Only naturally occurring fertilizer, like manure may be utilized to raise organic produce. While it's still better to eat non-organic veggies than no veggies at all, consumers are beginning to see the value in organic products.

The natural and organic skin care product sector has seen an increase of 39 % over the last year. The product preparations rely completely on natural or naturally derived ingredients. These products don't utilize any artificial preservatives.

The FDA doesn't regulate skin care manufacturers, questionable ingredients frequently make their way into their formulas. A few of these products might claim to be all natural, while still bearing a slew of chemicals and toxins. As a consumer if a skin care product bears an ingredient that you're unsure about, write down its name and do some research. If a product claims to be all natural, its ingredients ought to be easily recognizable as natural elements.

Scrutinize the first several listings in the product to be certain that they're the natural ingredients you're seeking. Dirt, dust, pollutants, and other environmental pollutants enter the body through the skin, supplying a more significant gateway to your system, so it's crucial to be aware of what products contain. In response to a growing requirement on the part of consumers, more and more organic foods and products are swamping the market. Even in mainstream supermarkets, certified organic foods and organic skin care products are available.

Demand for organic production is increasing by at least forty percent every year. And while in a few cases the price for organic raw materials can be three to four times more expensive than conventional. If consumer demand grows, prices ought to continue to fall.

Chapter 2:
Nutrition And Organics

Synopsis

In our pursuit for a healthier life-style and following a better more nutritious diet, we're occasionally faced with choices. Is it better for me to buy natural, organic and hormone free foods? What do these things mean?

What's The Nutritional Value

When you head to the food market, shopping for products like eggs, meat, fish, milk, and produce may be very tricky. Signs are posted all over the place labeling food as natural, organic, and a number of additional things—but what's the difference, truly? Learning what particular names mean may help you choose if you ought to dole out additional money on a product, whether the nutrition value is better or if it's simply a promotion ploy.

Natural is a term affiliated with a number of fruit and veggie products. Commonly, this is simple a promotion ploy to convince you to purchase the product. After all, all fruits and veggies are natural, correct? Unless it's a new sort of food that has been developed and processed, the product is natural. In all likelihood what you're truly looking for is organic. Organic foods are grown without chemical pesticides and fertilizers.

There are 2 main advantages with organic foods. First of all, you're helping the environment, as chemicals are not being put in to nature. Second, you are avoiding consuming chemicals and are consequently benefitting by utilizing a healthier food.

All the same, organic products are commonly more expensive while nutrition is the same (I mean a great apple is a great apple). If you're on a budget, skip over organic fruits and veggies that you have to peel, like oranges and bananas. After all, once you've cast aside the peel, you've likewise discarded the chemicals. Instead, opt for organic items like apples, where you eat the peel. Regardless what you purchase, all the same, make certain that you rinse off the food when you get home.

A different tricky label you will see is "no hormones." This is commonly in regards to milk or meat products and is false, as all animals naturally produce hormones. Hormones are what helps an animal (even a human being) regulate body organs, have young and otherwise function. All meat products have hormones. What the labels truly mean is that no hormones were artificially given to the animal, which is occasionally done to step-up milk production. Regardless of hormones, all the same, the milk and meat is safe for an individual and not a violation of an animal's rights.

Lastly, a label on eggs and meat may indicate if the animal was caged or penned. This doesn't make a difference in the quality or nutritional value of the meat, but is merely a matter of animal rights. These products might be a bit more expensive, but if you want to make humane decisions, that's the way to go.

Reading the label and arriving at healthy choices may occasionally be hard, but learning how to do so may help you make the most beneficial decisions for your diet.

Chapter 3:
Organics And Your Health

Synopsis

Organic food is food that's free from all genetically modified organisms, developed without artificial pesticides and fertilizers and derived from an animal raised without the routine utilization of antibiotic drugs, growth boosters or additional drugs. Once only found in small stores or farmers' markets, organic foods and other products are getting to be much more broadly available.

Health

Organic foods have been proven to better your immune system, help you sleep well, shed the extra weight more easily, and better your blood work just to name a few. Organic food may boast intense, realistic flavors, and an elevated vitamin and mineral content in some instances.

And though logically it makes sense to eat a diet based on organic foods, a few worry about the cost. However with measured planning and preparation, going organic is really rather affordable. And, the peace of mind knowing you and your loved ones are eating foods that haven't been processed with pesticides or genetically altered is worth the additional money spent.

The pesticides utilized by conventional farmers may have a lot of damaging influences on your health, including neurotoxicity, disruption of your endocrine system, carcinogenicity and immune system suppression.

Pesticide exposure might likewise affect male reproductive function and has been associated to miscarriages in women. In addition, conventional produce tends to have fewer nutrients than organic produce. On the average, conventional produce has only eighty-three percent of the nutrients of organic produce. Studies have detected significantly elevated levels of nutrients such as vitamin C, iron, magnesium and phosphorus, and significantly less nitrates (a toxin) in organic crops.

So it's a bright idea to purchase and eat organic produce and free-range organic foods as much as possible for utmost health benefits. Additionally, the knowledge that you're supporting the organic foods industry that is dedicated to protecting the environment by steering clear of adverse pesticides and chemicals that may result in the loss of topsoil, toxic runoff and resulting water pollution, soil pollution and poisoning and the death of insects, birds, critters and advantageous soil organisms ought to help you feel even better.

Chapter 4:

Organic Skin Care

Synopsis

The organic skin care tendency has been getting a lot of attention in recent years. This chapter provides a definition for organic skin care. It likewise talks about a lot of key benefits of utilizing organic skin care products and how it may benefit the user, the environment, and the economy.

For The Skin

If there's one beauty trend that appears to be getting its fair share of attention and hype, it is organic skin care. A lot of individuals, especially celebrities, are switching over to organic skin care products and letting other people know about it. Before passing off organic skin care as simply some Hollywood trend, read on for more info about it and why switching to it may be the most beneficial thing you'll ever do for your skin.

What does organic skin care imply?

Organic simply implies that no chemicals were utilized in the manufacturing of a product and in growing the elements that comprised it. Organic skin care products are made without utilizing any preservatives, chemicals, or other synthetic materials. They're made of natural ingredients like blossoms, herbs, fruits, nuts, milk, and oils that are cultivated without the utilization of pesticides, commercial fertilizers, and possibly toxic substances.

Advantages of switching to organic skin care

Organic skin care products work as simply as well or even better than conventional skin care products. There's likewise a wide choice of organic skin care products that may cater to your beauty needs. From lotions and creams to lip balms and lipsticks, there's an organic skin care product that may suit you. Utilizing organic skin care products benefits not only you but others and the environment likewise. Below are a few of the key advantages of changing over to organic skin care:

- Enhanced health

Studies demonstrate that almost 60% of chemicals found in conventional commercial skin care products and cosmetics find their way into the bloodstream. While trace amounts of these chemicals might not pose significant threat, an accumulation may be potentially toxic. By utilizing organic skin care products, you do away with the risk of chemicals oozing into your bloodstream.

- Lower pollution

Apart from contributing to your wellness, the utilization of organic skin care products likewise decreases pollution. Conventional cosmetics and skin care products are mass-produced in big factories and labs utilizing different preservatives and chemicals.

Manufacturing by-products are disposed off as liquid waste or discharged as fumes. These waste materials may potentially harm the environment. On the other hand, organic products are cultivated and manufactured without utilizing any chemical or preservative in cautiously controlled conditions designed to maintain the natural attributes of the ingredients.

- Bettered economic system

You likewise help improve the country's economic system by supporting organic skin care products. Manufacturers of organic products are commonly small-scale businesses while their suppliers are proponents and practitioners of organic farming. By supporting organic skin care products, you support and step-up the demands for their business.

Organic skin care utilizes Mother Nature's natural beautifiers to keep your skin supple and healthy. Simply be certain to consult your physician prior to trying any skin care product, whether it's organic or not.

If you're interested in utilizing organic skin care products, it's wise to be knowledgeable of the requirements and standards set by the USDA for organic skin care products to guarantee their quality.

Chapter 5:
Choosing Organic Skin Care Products

Synopsis

The increasing popularity of organic skin care has paved the way for the manufacture of a wide assortment of organic skin care products. This chapter supplies insight and info about organic skin care products along with tips on selecting true and quality organic products.

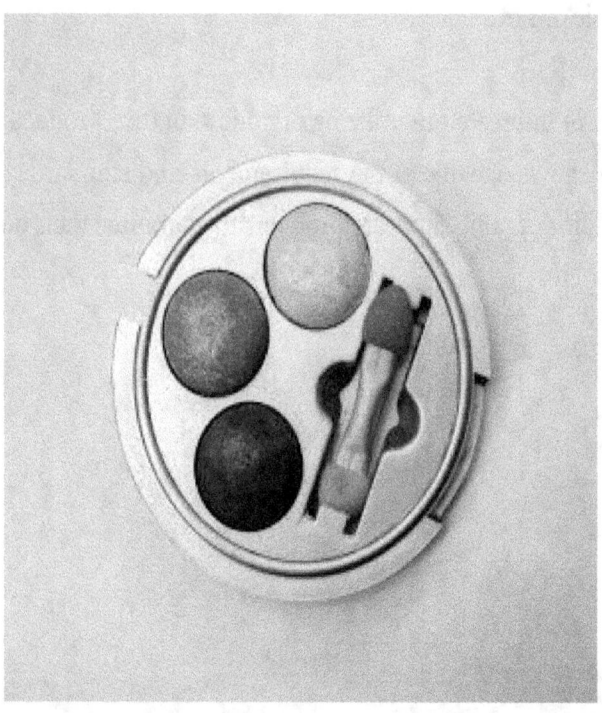

Tips On Choosing

Take a stroll along any beauty or skin care aisle and you'll be bombarded by products laying claim to the fact that they're "all-natural" or "organic." The high demand for organic skin care products has driven major skin care product and cosmetic manufacturers to mass-produce.

Regrettably, while this seems like great news, mass producing skin care products and cosmetics isn't pragmatic unless manufacturers utilize preservatives and additional chemicals to increase the shelf life of their supposedly "organic" products. As such, care has to be taken in selecting organic skin care products to assure authenticity and quality. Here is a guide to help you in selecting true organic skin care products:

1. Look for the Department of Agriculture organic seal of approval.

The Department of Agriculture has imposed a lot of requirements for organic skin care products. Each product claiming to be organic has to bear the Department of Agriculture organic seal of approval. This means that the product has been examined and had met the quality criteria set by the Department of Agriculture for safety.

The Department of Agriculture sign means that the product and its elements have passed tests conducted by the Department of

Agriculture for antibiotic and hormone utilization in livestock and crops.

2. Go beyond face-value.

Don't take the manufacturer's word for what it is. As an alternative, read the label to get a thorough idea of the components used for the manufacture of the product. If manufacturers place "organic" or "all-natural" labels on their products, they may be stretching the truth a little.

A few unscrupulous manufacturers might have used an organic ingredient however this doesn't make their products "organic." Instead, check and read labels thoroughly to see to it that the product you are going to purchase is indeed organic. Whenever possible, take note of some components you don't understand in the label and look it up online before your purchase to assure that they are not preservatives or chemicals.

3. Be acquainted with Department of Agriculture organic ranking.

The Department of Agriculture grants its organic seal of approval to products that cleared its organic standards. In addition, the Department of Agriculture likewise implements a system that specifies a product as purely organic or not. Being familiar with this system assures that you won't be fooled when it comes to selecting an organic product. First of all, only products that utilized purely organic substances in their manufacture may be labeled "100% organic." Next, products with 95% or more organic components may be labeled "organic" in their primary label. Following, products with 70%-95% organic components may only be described as "made with organic components" with 3 of these organic components listed on the label. Finally, products with merely 70% organic components or less may only use the word "organic" in their ingredient section.

By comprehending what the manufacturers mean when they label their products as organic, you are able to minimize the risk of buying scam products masquerading as organic skin care lines. Better yet, research on the Net for reviews and recommendations on the most beneficial organic skin care products around to make your selection simpler.

Chapter 6:
Organic Bath Soaps

Synopsis

Instead of soaping up your body with harsh chemicals why not take time to learn why organic bath soaps are becoming the first choice for people all over the world. These organic bath soaps come from natural resources. The soaps and bath products will provide protection for your skin.

Soaps

Visit the Net where you'll find a nice assortment of organic bath soaps. A few of the soaps are hand carved and cold processed. These soaps are amazing for those individuals that battle sensitive skin. You are able to find liquid soaps, organic gel soaps, and non-toxic cleaners by shopping on the Net.

Shopping on the Net is smart as you have a broader selection of organic soaps to consider. You will discover natural blends, traditional blends, processed soaps, and so forth. Even if you have highly sensitive skin, you will discover organic soaps that will not bother your skin.

Organic soaps are healthier than a few of the shampoos, soaps, and so forth manufactured with all the extra unneeded stuff. A few of these soaps have harsh chemicals that link to particular types of cancers.

Check the ingredients on your shampoo or soap package and do an in-depth research on the Net to learn more about the chemicals in non-organic soaps, shampoos and so forth. This will help you appreciate how valuable organic soaps may be for you.

More and more individuals these days are going back to natural living. This is because they're finding out that fabricated products in most cases are not so great after all. Individuals are discovering that organic living is encouraging healthy skin, healthy hair, and longer life.

So be certain to check out the wide assortment of organic soaps online. You will find an assortment of soaps, Shea butter, primo incense, pet shampoo, skincare solutions, organic wash, organic horse shampoo and more.

See even your pet may get the benefits of living healthy and natural.

The organic soaps give you a mixture of water, alkali and oils. A few soaps likewise have glycerin mixed into the bar so that you have a moisturizing solution.

All ingredients are natural, coming from a few of the finest plants, tree life and so on. A few of the best organic soaps include the Aloe-Vera based soaps. Aloe Vera is an amazing natural source that will moisturize your skin.

Chapter 7:
What About Organic Gardening

Synopsis

Let's have a look at why you should grow our own organic veggie garden.

Growing Your Own

During the last decades, there has been a change toward automation and homogenization of farming, which uses pesticides, additives, herbicides, man-made fertilizers and mass-production strategies. All this is understandably affecting mankind's health, and new diseases are spreading quickly amongst human beings and animals (bird's flu being the most recent one).

The World Health Organization brings forth reports to show how the utilization of chemicals and additional products on food, coupled with the manufacturing procedures involved, are actually a threat for our health.

If you have space for a few pots or even a little piece of land, it is a sensible decision to grow your own organic veggie garden. Today I'm posing 7 reasons for doing this:

1. You'll have no additives in your veggies. Research by organic food associations has demonstrated that additives in our food may cause heart diseases, osteoporosis, migraines and hyperactivity.

2. There will be no pesticides or synthetic fertilizers utilized. These chemical products are applied to have bigger crops all the time regardless of blights or weather conditions, and affect the quality of the veggies. As well, pesticides are generally poisonous to humans.

3. Your veggies won't be genetically modified (GM). Antibiotics, drugs and hormones are utilized on veggies to grow more and bigger ones. One of the consequences of this practice is veggies which look all the same and are commonly don't taste as good. Besides, we end up consuming the hormones that have been utilized on the veggies, with the likely risks for our health.

4. Consuming your own organic veggies will be much healthier for you. They will not have any of the products or chemicals named above, and they'll be much more natural than any ones you would find at the supermarket. Your health won't be at risk, as you will then know that nothing has been added to your veggies.

5. Your own organic veggies will be much more mouth-watering. The utilization of pesticides, synthetic fertilizers, hormones and antibiotics make veggies grow unnaturally and take the taste away from them. With organic veggies, your cooking will be enhanced, as their flavor will show fully.

6. Organic farming is friendly to the environment. Because you won't utilize pesticides or additional equally harming products on your veggies, you will not damage the soil or the air with the chemical elements.

7. When you raise your own organic veggies you're contributing to your own self-sustainability and the sustainability of the planet. Small communities have been founded where members exchange products

that they grow naturally, therefore contributing to create a friendly and better place for us all.

In the end, consuming organic products only means that we don't add anything else to them than they would naturally have. As you are able to guess, additives, fertilizers, pesticides or hormones are not elements of naturally grown food. To better care for your health, grow your own organic veggies.

Chapter 8:

Tips For Organic Gardening

Synopsis

Organic gardening is the exact same as regular gardening except that no man-made fertilizers or pesticides are utilized. This may make particular aspects hard, like controlling disease, insects, and weeds. Organic gardening likewise requires more attention to the soil and the varied needs of plants.

Tips

Organic gardening begins with the soil. Gardeners have to add organic matter to the soil on a regular basis in order to keep the soil productive. As a matter of fact, compost is crucial to the healthiness and well-being of plants grown organically. Compost may be made from leaves, dead blossoms, veggie scraps, fruit rinds, grass clippings, manure, and a lot of other things.

The ideal soil has a rich color, sweet smell, and is full of earthworms. Some soil might need more natural additives than regular compost may give, like bone meal, rock phosphates, or greensand. A simple soil test will tell you the pH balance and which nutrients you'll have to utilize.

One circumstance that makes even gardeners that are really serious about organic gardening reach for pesticides is bugs on their plants. The most beneficial way to defend plants against bugs is to take preventative measures.

One thing that may be done is to make certain plants are healthy and not too wet or dry as bugs commonly attack unhealthy plants and if healthy, they may frequently outgrow minor insect damage. An assortment of plant types is a great idea to keep pests of a certain plant type from taking out the whole garden.

Possibly the best way to defend against bugs is to make your garden alluring to insect predators, like ladybugs, birds, frogs, and lizards. You may do this by keeping a water source nearby or by raising plants that draw in insects who feed on nectar. Other ideas are sticky traps, barriers, and plant collars. There are a few household items that prevent against insects as well, like insecticidal soaps, garlic, and hot pepper.

To avoid plant disease in organic gardening, select disease resistant plants and plant them in their prime conditions. A lot of diseases will spread because of constant moisture and bad air circulation, so the site of your garden and the way it's watered may help ensure against diseases.

Weeds may be a bothersome and frustrating part of organic gardening. Organic mulch may act as a weed barrier, but for even better protection place a layer of newspaper, construction paper, or cardboard under the mulch.

Corn meal gluten will slow the development of weeds if spread early in the season prior to planting, as does solarization. There's as well the old-fashioned art of hoeing and hand pulling that always works.

Your best bet in weed prevention is perseverance. Mulch well and pull and hoe what you may; after a few seasons you may beat the weeds permanently.

Organic gardening is an excellent way to assure that your plants will be free and clear of all pesticides and, if attended to properly, will be as healthy as possible. Organic gardening might take a bit more time and care than regular gardening, however after gardeners get the hang of it and work out all the quirks of their garden, it's definitely worth the additional time.

Wrapping Up
Final Words

Besides the fact that organic food tastes better and it cuts down the amount of cancer-causing chemicals that go into your body, there are plenty of other really great reasons why you ought to purchase organic food. Here are just a few:

The animal from which you got your meat is assured to have been healthy throughout its life. How come? Part of the criteria governing organic products is agreeing not to utilize antibodies to treat a sickness. Animals that are raised with the elemental goal of being organic are raised in more humane conditions (as outlined by the U.S.' Humane Society).

These better living situations result in healthier animals and healthier animals merely are less prone to sickness and disease. Naturally, nothing may guarantee an animal will never get sick, and from time to time one will require antibiotics to heal an ailment.

When this set of circumstances occurs however, the animal that was treated with the antibiotics have to be removed from the organic farm. The affected animal loses its organic position and is commonly sold to a conventional farm where it lives out the balance of its life.

If you purchase organic food, you're basically making a statement that you care about what you're placing into your body. So much is happening to our food before it goes in the supermarket. We hear about it, yet we do nothing to stop it. If you ever took a couple of minutes to consider all that food is exposed to, from beginning to end, the details probably would boggle your mind.

Sure, all that perfectly-shaped produce and those quite full-sized chicken breasts look tempting, however those perfections are the end result of growth hormones, gene-splicing, and an abundance of pesticides and fertilizers.

You've likely heard the saying, "Nature isn't perfect" countless times, yet again and again you continue to reach for that perfect tomato. If you buy organic, you're in effect stating you don't want to be part of that scene anymore. When enough individuals buy organic, and more are making the switch each day, food companies will be forced to hear consumers.

The chemicals that go onto the fields that produce the fruits and veggies you eat and that feed the cows and pigs that turn into your burgers and pork chops pollute the soil and the water. This impacts the animals that live off the land and it likewise pollutes the environment. If you select foods that are produced without these cancer-causing chemicals, you're not adding to this issue. Your purchases likely won't put an end to environmental harm, however as with all things in life, change starts with one human. Get a few acquaintances to alter their buying and eating habits, and then have them get a few acquaintances to switch and before long, a sizeable impact will be in the works.